An account of the hand Of God.

By Susan Blad

For my family; husband, brothers, sister, father and mother, and other mother. For my children, William, Johnathan, and Melissa, thank you for Your loving support. For my brother Gary who took the time to assist and teach me the art of self-publishing. And for Louis Bell, who mentored me through the most crucial part of God healing me.

TABLE OF CONTENTS

Forward

My Orphaned heart

I sought to fill the aching space
That only God can fill,
With things and people and
Suffered even more.
I sought to find peace and comfort
In another's touch,
but only reaped corruption
As a bounty for my hear.
While God stood watching
With arms open wide.
Calling me by name
That in him I might abide.
But my heart could not imagine
That he could be my worth,
Or that he bought my soul
By spilling his blood into my dirt.
The still small voice of love
Is all I can hear.
It washes away the condemnation
Of what comes to my ears,
And seeks to fill the aching space
I once sought to fix.
Once my heart was orphaned, empty
And void of loving life, until
Life itself came to be my guide.

Part 1. My testimony in a nutshell plus poetry

People have said that I was stuck for a while, but they do not understand that I was stuck from the age of 6 ½ yrs. Experience has taught me that most people do not understand the impact of sexual abuse. It changes that persons' life forever, alters everything about them. It steels their identity and opens that person to a type of fear that paralyzes their life. Maturity comes with great struggle because their heart becomes orphaned. That person feels as though they do not fit anywhere, and they become afraid of everything. They struggle to see themselves as being loveable or able to trust and give love. Life becomes a living hell filled with shame and guilt. This was me, until the Lord began to restore what was lost.

People encouraged me to work, but I had no emotional capacity to deal with people. I just stayed stuck and emotionally incapacitated for most of my adult years.

First, I sought help through counselors and doctors, but after decades of getting no place I gave up, they just labeled me and gave out bottles of pills. Every time I mentioned my childhood pain, I was told that I just needed to get over it, that it is in the past. The event took place in past years, but I lived with it every minute of every day. Scenes of the acts of abuse ran before my eyes like a movie through my waking hours. All those symptoms have a root that usually is extremely deep, the only way to move on with life is to walk through the issues from the root. They cannot be ignored, or gone around, they must be worked through.

Change came into my life when I began listening to a Christian radio station. My life took a turn that has brought me to where I am today.

Twenty-three years of seeking out people to help me, was finally over. The lord began to clean my heart with his love and sent a few people who embraced me into their lives.

I have always loved Jesus but had no clue that I needed to accept that he died for my sin and that I could go be with him when I have finished my time on earth. I believe the emotional pain was so loud that I missed a lot of my life. I was robbed by a thief in the night and restored by the son of God, and the light.

I do not share much about my life before I gave it to the Lord because it was exceedingly difficult. I grew up with a lot of abuse, I was an angry depressed teen-ager and spent those years trying to commit suicide. Then I married at the age of 18, believing that I had no skills to care for myself and needed someone to take care of me; and not realizing that I was doing this to get out of the house. Life was not easier in a marriage with a guy who only thought about his needs. It was like going from the frying pan to the fire. I was just a kid, an angry bitter person who had no sense of what life is or what it is to love. I did not know how to resolve the ache in my gut or to give another person what they need, so my life just kept getting harder.

The Crushing

Many are the
Afflictions of the
Righteous,
But God will deliver me
Out of them all.
Yet I am
Pressed from every side,
Crushed with circumstances.
Cast down but not
Destroyed.
Forgotten but not forsaken
Rejected, depressed
And beaten down, but not
Defeated.
Many are my afflictions,
But my God
WILL
Deliver me out of them all.
With him I stand
Without him I fall.

Even though just a year earlier I had decided that having children would not be a healthy event for me, I allowed my husband to talk me into having a child. Then two years later I wanted another, when he was eighteen months old, I was having my third child.

It was not until decades later that I realized we live with every decision we make. They pile up and produce growth in our lives, whether it is a plant with good effects or a weed, it grows until the garden of our lives are weeded out. Mine was overgrown with thistles. They appeared to have giant thorns that stuck me every time I moved. Matthew 7:24-29

Blind as a bat

I was blind as a bat,
Running around not knowing
Where I was at.
Meeting others needs
While my own were neglected.
Facing their life with all my strength
While mine is a mess and completely rejected.
Emptiness and pain chew away at my
Sleep,
Eat at my health and leave me dejected.
Oh but who is to blame
Only myself for not taking the reins.
For not seeking direction.
Life is too short and much too precious
To continue living without
And not being introspective.
Here come the corrections
A complete change of direction.
Pardon me if I step on your toes
For what I shall do only
God knows.
To fulfill his plans I may seem harsh
But whose eternity
Will be left in the dark. Only my own
If I do not hearken to the voice
in my heart.

My thistles were easy to identify; they were unforgiveness, bitterness, anger, anxiety, and depression. Identifying them was the easy part, it quickly became obvious that I had no idea or skill for how to overcome them. They poisoned every relationship I had and made my life a living hell.

That is until one afternoon I was listening to a Christian radio station in my car. The pastor gave a prayer to commit ones' life to the Lord. At first, I said the prayer in my mind, but the pastor stopped and, said "some of you are saying this in your head, you need to speak it out loud." For me it was like a light bulb came on and I repeated the prayer out loud. The presence of God came into the car and I began to weep. I have never been the same since that day. (John 3:16 God so loved the world, that he gave his only begotten son, that whosoever believeth in him should not perish, but have everlasting life.)

Just a Dream?

It was just a dream I thought,
Or was it?
I was running through the
House,
Trying to escape.
But every were my feet Went
Love met me in that place.
And when the hurt
Was beyond expression,
Love came
With open arms.
Everywhere I turned
Love was in my Face,
It went beside me, it was
Behind.
And ran out in front of me
To prepare the way.
It was just a dream I thought,
But how could this Be?
There is just one kind of Love
That seeks the heart like this,
The kind that gave
His life for me,
and died
Upon the tree.

By this time, I was two years into my second marriage, and it really was not any different than the first one because I did not know how to be married. Love was like an illusion to me, I thought it was that fuzzy feeling in my chest. Had no idea that love is commitment, love is forgiveness. I once read that the woman sets the tone of the marriage, yuck, I would hate to admit that now. My tone was everything but love and forgiveness. All I knew was fear, depression, and anxiety. After all I was the one who had a complete nervous breakdown at the age of 26 and spent 8 years going in and out of mental health wards. I was the one who had 29 shock treatments in a three-year period. But I was also the one who came to the end of myself and put my trust in God. So maybe there is a chance to live free and know how to love.

The Shattering

It was so complete that there was
Nothing left
Of me.
I had to start over
On unfamiliar ground,
With nothing left to lean
On, but the one
Who saved my soul. All of me
Was broken in pieces on the floor.
But in my weakness
Your strength
Came shining through.
Mending all my Shattered
Places and my thinking too. Giving
Beauty for ashes, the garment of praise
For the spirit of heaviness, but there
Is one thing that I know. It is
Your love that seems
To be the glue.
That shapes a
Shattered life
Into so much beauty, like a pillar
In your kingdom
And a vessel you can use.

It took many years for me to heal, and in the process my second marriage got abusive also. He even began to persecute me for my faith. There was screaming and pounding a lot of the walls. I went to the prayer closet, while I was in there sobbing and praying, I heard a still small voice come from the depths of my heart. The voice was so soft and gentle as it released me from the marriage, but in my 51 years I had never worked outside of my home. I took a part time position at an alterations shop for the prom and spring wedding season and spent a total of nine months saving every penny I earned. It felt as though my heart was ripped from my chest. I could not sleep for fear that he would kill me. Six months after the Lord released me from the relationship, my husband told me to move out. It was easy to blame both of my ex-husbands for the

failure of the marriages, though they had a larger part in what happened, I could not heal until I took responsibility for myself. It is impossible to give unconditional love out of a broken heart, the realization of my situation came tumbling down. I knew that what I needed was to sit still and let God finish healing me.

Broken Commitments

I renounce the wedding vows
Made before his face,
To lie in some dark back
Room with the rings of
His choice.
Where yellow gold
And diamond chips
Are chosen just for scraps.
There they lie in silence as
Tokens of my past.
I renounce all connection
And emotion of my will,
That bound me in relationship
With abuse and his control.
I renounce the tenderness
Given just to him.
That seemed only to
Draw criticism and caustic tongues
That cut the heart of me.
There is just a heap of dust
Lying at my feet, shaken from
The life I once thought I had.
With symbols of the lies we lived
Stripped and used for scraps,
Lying in some dark back room
Remaining In my past.

There was relief, and light at the end of the tunnel, but I still had to tell my family what was going on. It turned out that I was deceiving myself. I never said a word about the marriage, but my family saw how he treated me. When I told my siblings, each one said, "it's about time you get out of there." One brother sent me money to help get out of the house. He has been a light in my life his whole life.

The Christian friends we had were another story. Most of them stated that there is no provision for divorce in the Bible. Many stated that I had to stay in the marriage no matter how bad he treated me. But every time I opened the bible God lead me to scriptures that reaffirmed his original word of release from the marriage. Most of those "friends" abandoned me when I moved out on my own. I settled into life that felt absent from fellowship of those whom I had grown close to and served the Lord with. My focus quickly changed to becoming as close to the Lord as I could get, seeking work and trying not to focus on the heap of pain in my life.

As the winter worn on, I found myself working in a small alterations shop. I began to sense changes taking place within my own thinking.

Not as it seems

From deep inside a
Whisper came.
It could not be stopped
From its refrain,
It is March I heard loud
And clear.
The deadest time of the year,
Trees appear like sticks
Poking from
Gray brown dirt. Prairie
Grass blows dry
And brittle in
The last of winter's wind.
But the call of songbirds
Can be heard,
As tree sap begins to flow.
The barren earth
Warms in the sunshine.
So, all is not as it appears
Nor can one know the heart
Emerging from its
Winter place,
Heaped about with dirt
And disgrace.
Winds chafing the battered edges,
Who can know what is deep inside
Where the spirit God Loves to hide.

When time came to move out, I found myself in a little apartment across town. There I had to face myself and everything that had happened to me through my 51 years. The journey God brought me on has no words to describe. He was there every minute. I had no job, he sent people who gave me money when my stash ran out. One of which came to my door with an envelope packed with 20-dollar bills. Then he gave me a part time job and alimony. Most of all he gave me a place to heal. Then a few years later He gave me full time work and a bigger nicer place to live.

The Cocoon

I feel like a butterfly
Breaking free from
A wooly cocoon.
Stunned by the sights and
Sounds of a brand new
Life.
A freedom
Found in the wind
Beneath the wings.
The majesty of the butterfly
Is seen fluttering through the
Summer winds,
Arrayed with colors they
Dart to and fro in the
Freedom gained in a tight
Cocoon.
The place of transformation,
The place
Where one state dies
Only to give way to
The beauty of
The butterfly.

Facing myself was difficult, but I could not move on until I accepted myself with all my faults and limitations. Accepting what happened to me was the next step, I prayed and cried and finally was able to see that what happened had nothing to do with me. God gave us free will because he wants us to choose to worship him, but some people get deceived by the devil and choose to use their free will to be destructive to themselves and innocent people around them. Accepting what happened made it easier to let it go and severed the hold it had on my identity. Then it was easy to let go of the people who sexually abused me. I began to see them as victims and praying for them came easy because there was compassion in my heart. I have witnessed the Lord restore the person who did the most damage to my life (not my father), and I have witnessed God restoring and setting free my father. These relationships are better than they have ever been, they are like nothing ever happened.

The Healing

I had to come full circle
Returning to the special
Place we once shared.
To find out who I am,
To sprint the plains of
Self-deception
And climb the mountains of blindness.
To live in the valley
With hands raised, understanding
The painful reality of life.
I had to come full circle to experience
You again.
To feel the warmth of your embrace
Carry away the pain of
My past.
I had to come full circle
Receiving once again the wounds
You suffered,
The grace you offer,
To lay aside
Who I used to be I had to
Come circle
To surrender me.

People ask how God healed me; the answer is
always the same. I soaked myself in his word until
it became a part of who I am, I spoke scriptures
over myself that applied to situations in my life.
My mindset changed from that of a victim of abuse
to believing that I have a purpose, I am loved, I am
chosen, I have great value, I am a child of god; this
is who God's word says I am.

The Tongue

When I was a little kid
My heart was very
Tender.
Mama used to teach me
That sticks and stones
Could break my
Bones,
But names could never
Hurt me.
As I have grown
I've come to
Know that words can be very cutting.
Much more hurtful than a
Broken leg or being
Hit by an
Angry person.
Words go deep to the inner
Most part of us, lodging themselves
Like arrows in the heart and mind.
They cripple and maim
Or they can heal and
Sooth the wounds
Of an enemy.
They produce death or life
Whichever might be the intent,
Of the power
On the tongue.

I used to wonder how God could restore a life when it was broken from the beginning, but then it occurred to me that God knew everyone of us before He formed us in the womb. He knew us as complete and whole and that's how he can restore us to be someone we never were before.

My healing came without people laying hands on me, God does things the way he knows we will receive him. For the first few years of my salvation, I was in every prayer line there was offered. Then someone called me a spiritual piggy, my heart was so pierced by that statement, I just wanted to be healed. From then on, I sat before God in my own time, and He began to visit me during my personal worship time. He began to come sit with me when I patted a chair and invited his presence.

(Jeremiah 1:5 Before I formed ye in the belly I knew thee; and before thou camest forth out of the womb I sanctified thee, and I ordained thee a prophet unto the nations.)

Society VS the Lover of My Soul

In the scope of human thinking
My life looks like a total Waste.
Young years
Spent changing diapers, and Birthing
Children whom I would not
Raise.
In the scope of society
There I have no
Worth to spare.
No mark to make, no equivalence to Share.
But there is a place of one I Know,
Who treasures me as I am and
Does not judge who I
Used to be.
There sits the lover of my Soul.
The one who wipes my
Tears away, and in his
Comfort causes me to
Stay.

Part 2. Living out the healing plus poetry

Two years after I got out on my own the Lord gave me a dream and put it on my heart that his plan was for me to experience another marriage. At first my attitude was "no way," but the Holy Spirit wooed my heart and I gave my will over to him. The hardest part was the fear that after two years the relationship would become abusive just like before. I was single for a total of nine years without dating or getting into any kind of relationship. During those nine years I focused on putting my life in order, strengthening my relationship with God, and working. The Lord was with me directing my path and preparing my heart for his plan.

Still there was some fear even when I met my husband. At first, I told him to go away when he started talking about marriage, but he kept texting me with encouraging words. It only took five days for me to relent and say yes. While moving through that season, I realized the marriage was the completion of the healing. It took time for me to adjust and to surrender myself to the process, then a whole new world opened.

I have never known a relationship with a person who just loves me without expecting anything in return. He loves my heart instead of what he can get from me; he loves me with the God kind of love. So when I think of my life now, all I can say is that I am a walking miracle. A far-cry from the depressed terrorized person I was most of my life. Thank you, Jesus, I am eternally grateful.

God gave me poems as an outlet over the years, they are expressions of emotions, or relationships. Some are a revelation of a dream, many of them chronicle the journey God brought me through. I have enclosed some of them as expressions of this journey.

I believe that there will always be some needed healing in my life because we are never completely whole until we pass and stand before God. My garden is filled with roses now, it is a place where I meet with the Lord. The refreshing of His love is something I still cannot describe, but we share a communion that is filled with life and love.

If you have not accepted that Jesus died for you, to wash away your sin and heal your life please do. He loves you and wants you with him. Our eternity is a choice, God does not send us anywhere. We do it with our choices, our deeds and refusing to accept what Jesus did for us, because we want to be in control. Please take the way out that God has provided.

Choose to walk with him, seek him and you will find him. Read the first two chapters of book of Ephesians and write down what it says about you and you will find your identity in Christ. Allow God to lead you to a church and an older Christian who is willing to mentor and teach you. Most of all live out what God has given you. Gaining a healing or knowledge is the first part of walking with God. Walking in that knowledge and healing is what will change you forever. Trust God to lead you, seek his direction and walk it out. God Bless you and keep you and shine his face upon you. (Jeremiah 29:11 For I know the thoughts that I think toward you, saith the Lord, thoughts of peace, and not of evil, to give you an expected end.)

Part 3. Poetry

What do you do?

What do you do when everything
About your life
Is trained
To relate to the
Oppressor?
When your mind is trapped
Thinking about
All the
Abuse that has happened
To you, what
Do you
Do?
Where do you go for freedoms sake
how do you act
When love
Comes around?
Will you even recognize it?
Or turn your heart
The other
Way,
To relate to the familiar
Instead of the
Holy one?

The Transition

What will you do when
This transition is over,
When you live in a place
Without turmoil?
What will you do with
The time you have,
In the place where the
Other end of the rubber-band
Is flapping in the wind?
Will silence engulf your mind
And breed the peace of God?
Or keep you from yourself and
All the dreams that urge you on.
Will you set aflame the bridges
That could take you back.
What will you do with
This transition?

The Inner Chamber

There is an inner chamber
Where I dwell with my people.

There is an inner place, a womb
Of spiritual nature.

There is an inner chamber
Where rivers yearn to run,
To carry you from the natural
To a place you have never come.

There is an inner chamber
Where the voice of God cries out.
A place of holy nature
Where no flesh can go.

There is an inner chamber
A holy sanctuary.
Where the presence of his
Being overtakes what's in the way.

There is an inner chamber
Sown as a seed, a precious
Gift that is given when you come
To your knees.

Hindsight

I saw it in the distance
Howling like a hurricane, trolling to and fro
Calculating its'
Path and the treasure
It would know.
I heard you say
This is the calm before
The storm, but I did not get it, till
It turned with force
And headed straight for me.
In full view of all the people
And everyone we knew,
But they didn't
Seem to See
The truth or hear the
Shattered voice
That called for Recognition, and cried for
A better choice. but
Shunned the truth and Walked away
Leaving me Alone.
Now hindsight is 20/20
And life is never fair, leaving me
With answers when I've
Already been there.

Susan Blad Born January 15, 1953
In Glen Cove, Long Island, New York

AUTHOR:

My Orphaned Heart is an inspirational work that took a long time to put into its' final form. It is a written account of my very life; it is God's story through me. It chronicles the affect that abuses can have on the human spirit and the long journey experienced to finally come to peace with God and receive the healing He has in store for me.

Before I understood anything about God, (in 1989) I experienced a burning in my heart to tell my story. Someone gave a me typewriter that spent hours with my fingers banging on its' keys. I even submitted a chronological account of my life to a publisher. He returned it with a note stating that he had no place for such a sad story. Since then I tried to bury the story, tried to ignore it, and keep it to myself, but it will not leave me alone. The burning in my gut has only grown to become like a fire. God did such a miracle in my life; I must send His story through my life into the world. Maybe it will touch a life and encourage people to trust God to bring them through.

Within this story are poems the Lord gave me over the years He spent succoring my heart to place where I could trust him. They give a view of his work in my life. I take no credit for their content; they were neither pondered nor were they thought out. the words came into my heart and were written as I heard them.

The Bride

I saw myself in a meadow laughing and spinning
In the summer sunshine.
Wearing a long white wedding dress
With arms outstretched
Toward the sky.
The joy that filled my
Being emanated from all around.
Like the beauty of wildflowers swaying
In a meadow,
My feet danced with such
Precision. They were like the wind
Not knowing where they would
Travel next.
At first there seemed to be people
All about.
But as the music slowed,
It appeared the gaze I
Felt; was that of
The Lord
Loving watching
His bride.

Call to action

Foot Note

All scripture taken from the original King James Bible